Emotional Baggage

Mary Hale

www.WeAreAPS.com

Copyright © 2018 by Mary Hale

All rights reserved. No part of this publication may be reproduced, stored in a retrieval system, or transmitted, in any form or by any means, electronic, mechanical, photocopying, recording or otherwise, without the prior permission of the publishers.

ISBN: 978-1-945145-42-1

APS Publishing
2653 S. Lawndale
Chicago, IL 60623
847-942-6135
www.WeAreAPS.com

Table of Contents

Chapter 1..................................5
Cluttered Emotions

Chapter 2................................11
Understanding the Clutter

Chapter 3................................15
Emotional Beginnings

Chapter 4................................21
Emotions vs Feelings

Chapter 5................................27
Organizing the Clutter

Prayer....................................29

Reference
Notebook................................33

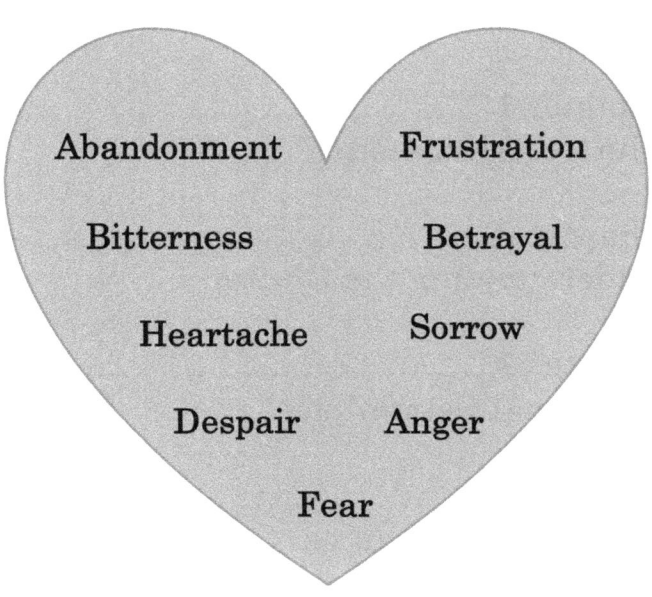

I CAN'T SEE WHAT MY HEART SAYS. I CAN ONLY FEEL THE PAIN…

Chapter 1:

Cluttered Emotions

Imagine never being able to walk in the destiny that was planned for us before we were consumed with regret, frustration, bitterness, and confusion. Or not knowing how much people care about us because we refuse to allow anyone to get close to us and know us, leaving family and friends with the legacy of not knowing who we truly are. I believe we all have something to offer each other and we all want to be loved.

Some of us have close family and friends that in the past may have been dear to our heart. However, due to the many bricks that have been thrown at us, we deal with anger and heartache. We build on those bricks of the past hurt and isolate ourselves from them. But we must be careful how we allow the pain to affect us and our future. Tomorrow is not promised.

A wall is an amusing thing; it can be your safety net. But, can you imagine having a heart-to-heart talk when one heart is free to express all its feelings and the other has a barrier around it with trapped emotions? Can you imagine having a conversation separated by a wall? The relationships and communication must be impossible.

If we could see each other's hurt or feel each other's pain, maybe we would understand why every day life has made us build up brick walls around our hearts. That is not going to happen, so until we as individuals release what is really going on, healing will never take place.

> "The heart is deceitful above all things and beyond cure. Who can understand it?"
>
> Jeremiah 17:9

The Heart Wall is the bricks or walls where the mind accumulates trapped emotions. The mind builds a wall around the heart with these emotions to protect the heart from being hurt or broken. To the mind, the wall is real.

We have a three-part entity in us – body, soul, and spirit. We are housed in a body on this earth, but when we are no longer in our body, what kind of legacy will we leave if we do not get pass the walls of our emotional baggage?

The soul becomes cluttered when we begin to worry and hold on to people and things that we should have let go. Things that were said or done to us in the past that were not a good experience. We relive our past traumatic experiences of what we encountered, and we don't allow anything or anybody to get near us to hurt us again. We make sure that our guards are in place because our mind holds on to the hurtful experience and our heart wall does not allow those painful things to repeat itself.

When we live our lives from a point of the past we can never enjoy our future. We live a life full of emotional clutter, it forms a barrier around the heart and it blocks our ability to give and receive love. There are no openings because the barriers are there to keep others from getting in. We keep those barriers up because we do not want to revisit whatever disappointment or trauma we lived in the past. Life becomes a little harder because we have a problem with letting people in, and for others to get close to us.

The barrier holds all our cluttered

emotions leaving our heart in captivity. This is what is known as a heart wall; there is no escape because there is no door. The fence, or barrier, is where the mind forms and processes our thoughts and holds the emotions that are trapped in our heart. Emotions we never released such as despair, betrayal, heartache, anger, bitterness, frustration, fear, sorrow, and abandonment.

We do not expect anything positive to occur from these barriers because of the clutter we hold from past experiences, so we have negative expectations or no expectations at all.

An example of clutter is what we put in our closet such as clothing, hats, and shoes we never wear. Things that still have tags on them from previous years. Paper items that we put in boxes that we never have time to read; these things just accumulate year after year. The clothes have dried and rotted, full of mildew and we don't bother to read the old papers. This is the same way that cluttered emotions accumulate in our soul.

Cluttered emotions form barriers of hopelessness, faithlessness, unhappiness, heartache, sorrow, grief, displeasure, hostility, resentment, frustration, a state of panic, regret, depression, neglect, being misused, and so on. These are just a few of the emotions that we hold on to.

Cluttered emotions enter our soul, which is our mind, will, emotions, personality, and our ego. The soul is the part that makes us who we are. If we never cross the barrier of being held captive, we suffer and our destiny is an altered state.

Chapter 2:

Understanding the Clutter

Visible Clutter

When clutter is visible, it distracts from the beauty of our individuality or our possibilities. It is like the clothes that no longer fit, but we keep them in our closet even though we have outgrown them. Or, like that big stack of mail or catalogs on the nice newly designed kitchen countertop – just looking at it becomes too much of a stressor because we continuously say, "Oh, I don't feel like dealing with this today. I will wait until tomorrow". However, tomorrow never comes so we leave it there.

Forgotten Clutter

There's also the forgotten clutter, like a pantry closet or kitchen cabinet that is seldom used. It has all the seasonings in the top cabinet; the cleaning products in the pantry have all expired and should have been thrown away, but for some reason we hold on to these things.

Soul Clutter

Soul clutter is the collection of emotional, relational, and spiritual issues we have been stepping over and ignoring. We ignore life situations and circumstances because they are too painful to give up or confront, or we fear that in coping with these issues we will have to surrender those thoughts that have consumed our lives.

Most of us think of a barrier as a safe place of escape, but in relationships, a barrier makes life a little uneasy. How can we have a true intimate conversation with anyone such as our mates, children, family, or friends? How can we kiss or hold someone we are supposed to love and admire when our heart is separated by cluttered emotions? It's not real love. Why? Because we never give all; we push people away.

How did some of these walls begin? They began with our ancestors – the roots or foundation of our family values and beliefs, eating habits, environment, and surroundings. Our lifestyle, our foundation, was laid by them and some of the things, if not all, have been passed on for generations. Some of them good and some not so good.

Think of it as a house. The roof is the lifestyle; the floor is the foundation; and one wall intersects with the other. Within those walls are our mind, body, soul, and intellect. Our intellect is our intelligence, reasoning, understanding, thoughts, senses, judgment, and wisdom.

This is our family structure – a combination of relatives, friends, etc. Some of us passed those beliefs that were handed down to us to our children, not truly understanding why these things were done or said. We simply did them because they were taught to us. I was raised under the "Do as I say and not as I do" rule. There was no explanation given. Many of the ways we communicate were even learned behaviors. Within our families, and among our friends, we may have been told that we would never amount to anything; that we were too skinny; too fat; etc. We took their opinions as fact, never questioning them, and repeated the methods.

Chapter 3:

Emotional Beginnings

The root is the source of our origin. The mind causes us to be aware of the world and the experiences that cause us to think and to feel. The body is the bones, flesh and organs. The soul is the spiritual part of a human. The walls are the hurt, deceit, and anger.

Our emotional beginning is the first relationship with our mother in her womb. We form a bond for those months, good or bad. This is our first love affair. We form a strong attachment because it makes us feel secure and loved. If we are rejected that security becomes a loss and we become fearful, which transitions into bitterness.

As adults, our family values and past experiences are there to prepare us for when we leave to live on our own. We bring those experiences into other relationships when we leave home. If we have experienced a bitter or traumatic lifestyle and we have not gotten released from that hurt, we have already formed emotional walls.

There are people, events and situations that some of us hold in our hearts that have traumatized us. Sometimes we hold our feelings in because we don't want to confront them. We become passive about life from words that were spoken over our lives or from situations and circumstances that have occurred throughout our lives.

We shut down from the things we feel we are most vulnerable to and we never release our trapped emotions. We are unable to leave the pain of yesterday and when we enter another relationship, we look to them to fix it and sometimes they have no idea of the barrier that surrounds our heart. Most times, we are the one with the problem.

Everyone has had an experience from the past that was not so pleasant. Everyone deals with their problems in different ways. We all have felt emotional pain at some point in life. I don't know of anyone that has said they have had a perfect life without any emotional setback. We are supposed to learn to love each day through our mistakes. If we never learn to love ourselves, we surely cannot forgive others because we are unable to let our heart heal.

We cannot hold on to bitterness and unforgiveness in our hearts. We have memory recall of those who were supposed to love us and did not. They either harmed us in some way through their actions or did not act in a loving way. We have lost someone or something that was close to us; it was a traumatic experience.

When we have traumatic experiences and do not allow the healing to take place, it brings on fear. Then we put up more barriers because we are afraid to show love. Fear brings on insecurity, which in turn causes us to prohibit others from entering our security zone for fear of being hurt again. So, we avoid any past pain by putting up our barrier to prevent the pain from recurring.

When we are fearful and insecure, we become angry; angry at ourselves for not being able to love, and angry at others for rejecting or misunderstanding our fears and insecurities. To defend our heart, we become angry because that person or thing becomes a threat to us. Fear, insecurity, and anger brings out hate. We hate ourselves and other people because we go through life experiencing emotional upsets, we are afraid to give love, whether it to family or friends. Often time, we hate ourselves because of all the emotional baggage we carry. We retaliate and become vengeful and begin to take out our disappointments and insecurities on others.

The way we act is a result our thoughts and beliefs, whether positive and negative, and all the insecurities and weaknesses that come with them, causing us to swing back and forth between hope and fear. Sometimes, we are so caught up in these barriers we forget that we have a future. We lose sight of who we really are, but we must remind ourselves not to dwell on all the bad things that have happened.

"I will give you a new heart and put a new spirit in you;
I will remove from you your heart of stone and give you a heart of flesh. And I will put my Spirit in you and move you to follow my decrees and be careful to keep my laws."

Ezekiel 36:26-27

Chapter 4:

Emotions vs. Feelings

What is the difference between emotions and feelings? Emotions are feelings we have, and feelings are sensations. We lust for the love and joy that others experience, but how can there be real love if we are unable to give love? What is the difference between love and lust? Love is positive, and lust fulfills a need.

When I was younger, I never understood the saying, "You're wearing your emotions on your sleeve"; but as I got older, it became very clear. The look on our faces and our actions sometimes make it very clear how we feel. Our feelings are visible before we act on them.

Our past disappointments can surely show up in our lives by our actions and responses. Sometimes life experiences can be hard, and we never forget what happened in past events in our lives – we hold on to those memories. We become captured by our own thinking.

We think that old things have faded away until something happens that remind us of the past. When emotional clutter shows up it's because our souls have never let go of the hurt, pain, and despair that we experienced from yesterday.

As adults, we don't understand why we react the way we do to certain situations, but in the back of our minds, we are held captive by the past events in our lives. We don't respond to other people as well as we would like to…we might say hurtful things. We can't seem to stay in a meaningful relationship and tend to isolate ourselves. We can't see where we are going because we keep looking at where we came from. This does not stop with us; we pass those very same feelings on to our children from our actions, just as our ancestors passed them on to us.

This kind of baggage can cause us to make the wrong decisions or no decision at all and can also cause physical as well as emotional damage in our lives. With that baggage comes depression, loneliness, abandonment, anxiety attacks, and a lot of other illnesses. This is the kind of clutter that leads to a lot of fear, false accusation, doubt, anger, hostility, discouragement, and disappointment.

As we go through life, we become isolated from our own selves. We never experience who we really are and what we can become, we pass up the opportunity of our great destiny and purpose in life that should have made us happy. Why? Because in our minds and hearts, we refuse to let go of the past and become fearful, which leads to our doubt of what we can do in life.

Fear is a reaction to an immediate threat. It is a feeling that we cannot control, but fear can sometimes protect us from making wrong decisions when it is used for the right purpose; otherwise, fear keeps us from exceeding in life. A sister to fear is worry. This is a choice we make regarding what to expect. If we have no expectation, we are stuck; if we do have expectation, we proceed with caution, which is good. However, we cannot allow fear and worry to overtake us.

Fear, false accusation, and

condemnation tells us that we will never amount to anything; we are not good enough; or we are a complete failure. It tears us down and crushes us into fragmented pieces. We can't pull ourselves together because we relive the past from fear and worrying what might happen, then our visions and dreams are shattered. We begin to think about our past failures and mistakes to justify how we feel about each situation in our present lives.

We are consumed with guilt, shame, doubt, judgment, unbelief, and hopelessness. These are things that hold us captive. Then, we start making excuses and blaming others, digging up the past to justify the future.

When we are imprisoned by our mind, we can never move forward because we can't see pass the doubt.

> "Casting down imaginations, and every high thing that exalteth itself against the knowledge of God and bringing into captivity every thought to the obedience of Christ."
>
> 2 Corinthians 10:5

Doubt causes us to be uncertain about life issues, then it becomes hard to make decisions because of fear and worry. Fear brings on anxiety, which means we anticipate something might happen that might be unpleasant in our mind because we start thinking about the possibility of something happening. We become so consumed with doubt that it becomes an obsession. In turn, that doubt transitions into disbelief, which then becomes a stronghold in our minds.

Chapter 5:

Organizing the Clutter

The hurt and damages are sometimes so hidden that they don't leave. If we have not forgiven ourselves and others, our memories stay formatted as we remember what happened in the past and react negatively to certain situations or circumstances. We sometimes do not understand why we react the way we do, and these responses can cause us to become angry and vengeful.
When we hold on to lies, even half-truths that were told to us in the past, we stop living in the present.

We bring past emotions into current relationships from something our family, friends, or lovers said years ago that influence the decisions we make today.

When someone rejects us, it doesn't mean we have to reject ourselves or dwell on the fact that because they think of us as less worthy that we will never find someone else that will love us for who we are. We must not lose sight of who we are. When we lose someone or something, we should never think of it as a loss because it is not lost. Whether it is a spirit or a material thing, we should hold on to the good times and the good things that were represented. Whether laughter or a keepsake that person or thing were gifts or life lessons to us at some point, so we can go on and better travel the path meant for us. There is a reason and season for everything we do here on earth.

Prayer

Father God, in the name of Jesus, I come to you today to ask you for forgiveness of anything I have said or done today as well as the past that was not like you. I ask you to wash it in the sea of forgetfulness. I realize I have held things in my heart that should have been long gone. I have said hurtful things to others out of ignorance and anger. I have lived through regret for some of the decisions I made. I ask you Lord for your mercy and grace to help me get beyond every hurtful situation and unlawful entry that I have left open to my soul so that my spirit can be free.

I command all generational curses that came from the root of my ancestors and every hereditary spirit operating in my life through curses, hexes and vexes to be bound and cast out. All spirits of lust, perversion, adultery, fornication, uncleanness, and immoral thoughts to come out that have entered in my mind and body. All spirits of hurt, rejection, fear, anger, wrath, sadness, depression, discouragement, grief, bitterness, and unforgiveness I want to come out of my emotional walls, so I may be free from all baggage that has gathered in my heart. I will live a healthy and prosperous life so that my children and grandchildren will have a life of good health and prosperity.

All spirits of confusion, forgetfulness, mind control, mental illness, double-mindedness, fantasy, pain, pride, and memory recall I command you to flee. I break, sever, and cut all curses of schizophrenia, depression, along with the root of bitterness to come out. All the spirits of stubbornness, disobedience, rebellion, self-will, selfishness, and arrogance to leave my will so that your will be done.

I command all spirits of addiction to come leave that may have entered through lust and greed; any and all spirits of witchcraft, sorcery, divination, and occult that may have been handed down from my ancestors to come out in the name of Jesus. All spirits operating in my head, eyes, mouth, tongue, and throat or any other passageway, I command you to come out. Lord, you said whatever we bind on earth would be bound in

Heaven. So, Lord, on this day I, bind every spirit of murder, suicide suicidal thoughts, premature and accidental death from me and my family so that we may live the life you have predestined us to live. I loose the spirit of love, joy and peace in Jesus name I pray. Amen, and it is so.

> "There is a right time for everything, and everything on earth will happen at the right time."
>
> **Ecclesiastes 3:3**

Reference Notebook

This section contains lists geared to help you become acquainted with various issues that may plague you. Once you identify the label that is attached to you, call it by name in your prayer so that you can be free.

THE WALLS OF DECEPTION

The source of deception is isolation, selectness, control, and false accusation. Deception is the doorway to our strongholds. It holds us captive and we perish from lack of knowledge.

THE DOORWAY

DECEPTION:

Confusion
Lying
Self-deception
Gullibility

The Problem:
"But you have planted wickedness, you have reaped evil, you have eaten the fruit of deception."
Hosea 10:13
New International Version

The Solution:
"...to root out, and to pull down, and to destroy, and to throw down, to build, and to plant."
Jeremiah 1:10
King James Version

LIST OF STRONGHOLDS

ABANDONMENT

Complaining
Critical Judging
Murmuring
Unforgiveness
Irrational Condemnation

ADDICTION:
Physical

Alcohol
Caffeine
Nicotine
OPIOD
Cocaine
Uppers/Stimulants
Marijuana
Any other street drugs
prescription drugs

ADDICTION:
Mental

Sex
Pornography
Masturbation
Gambling
Video Games
Television
Sports
Exercise
Other People
Receiving Attention

ANGER

Frustration
Hatred
Rage
Resentment
Temper
Bitterness
Tantrums
Spoiled Behavior
Feeling Bad Inside
Hidden Anger
(w/High Blood Pressure)

LIST OF STRONGHOLDS

ABANDONMENT

Complaining
Critical Judging
Murmuring
Unforgiveness
Irrational Condemnation

ADDICTION:
Physical

Alcohol
Caffeine
Nicotine
OPIOD
Cocaine
Uppers/Stimulants
Marijuana
Any other street drugs
prescription drugs

ADDICTION: Mental

Sex
Pornography
Masturbation
Gambling
Video Games
Television
Sports
Exercise
Other People
Receiving Attention

ANGER

Frustration
Hatred
Rage
Resentment
Temper
Bitterness
Tantrums
Spoiled Behavior
Feeling Bad Inside
Hidden Anger
(Associated w/High Blood Pressure)

ANXIETY

Burden
False Responsibility
Fatigue
Heaviness
Nervousness
Restlessness
Weariness

COMPETITION

Competitive when Driving
Jealousy Feelings
Possessiveness Feelings
Striving to out-do everyone
Pride
Competing when unnecessary
Competing with everyone and everything

CONFUSION

Confused Thoughts
Indecision
Lack of Focus
Lack of Concentration
Lapses in Memory
Inability to make conclusions
Distorted Perception
Hear Words That Aren't Said
Take things in a very
sensitive manner
Unable to grasp simple
truths

DEPRESSION

Feeling of Discouragement
Feeling of Despair
Feeling of Hopelessness
Self-pity
Over-Sleeping
Insomnia
Thoughts of Suicide
Suicidal Attempts
Withdrawing from Others

ESCAPE

Fantasizing
Lethargic Feeling
Passivity
Procrastination
Withdrawal from Others
Forgetfulness

FEAR

Agoraphobia – Fear of going outside
Genophobia – Fear of Sex
Cibophobia – Fear of Eating
Glossophobia – Fear of Talking
Vehophobia – Fear of Driving
Fear of Exercise
Ablutophobia – Fear of Bathing
Androphobia – Fear of Men
Gynophobia – Fear of Women
Philophobia – Fear of Relationships
Gamophobia – Fear of Commitment
Achievemephobia – Fear of Success
Theophobia – Fear of God
Anthropophobia – Fear of People
Ecclesiophobia – Fear of Church
Fear of Government

FINANCIAL PATTERNS

Greed
Stinginess
Spend too Much
Compulsive Shopping
Inability to Save
Inability to Budget
Live in Poverty
Job Losses
Poor Employment History

GREED

Cheating
Covetousness
Stealing
Misrepresentation
Fraud

GRIEF

Feeling of Loss
Feeling of Sadness
Feeling of Sorrow
Feeling of Suffering

INFIRMITIES/DISEASE

Arthritis
Asthma
Cancer
Diabetes
Fatigue
Fibromyalgia
Heart Disease
Hypertension
Migraines
Skin Diseases/Rashes
Premature Death
Physical Abnormalities
Sexually Transmitted Disease
High Blood Pressure

MENTAL ILLNESS

Feeling of Craziness
Compulsions
Confusion
Hallucinations
Hysteria
Insanity
Obsessive Compulsive
Schizophrenia
Paranoid
Seizures- All Types
Mental Anguish
Shock Treatments
Lobotomy

PRIDE

Arrogance
Self-Importance
Vanity
False Self-worth
Feeling Better Than Others
Plastic Surgery for Vanity Reasons
Criticizing One's Own Appearance
Disliking One's Own Race
Disliking One's Own Nationality
Criticizing Your Appearance

REBELLION

Stubbornness
Undermining
Lying
Insubordination
Argumentative
Hard Headedness
Debating

REJECTION

Perfectionism
Self-Rejection

SEXUAL SINS

Adultery
Fornication
Self Exposure
Homosexuality
Incest
Lesbianism
Fantasies of Lust
Pornography
Rape
Seduction
Sexual Abuse
Prostitution or Sex for Money
Sex with an Animal
Frigidity with Spouse

SHAME

Condemnation
Embarrassment
Guilt
Self-accusation
Self-Disgust
Self-Reproach

STRIFE

Arguing
Cursing
Dissension
Disagreement
Discord
Mocking
Blaming

UNBELIEF

Doubt
Disbelief
Rationalism
Skepticism
Unbelief
Doubt Everything
Trust Issues
Can't Believe Anything
Everything Seems Dubious

UNWORTHINESS

Feelings of Inferiority
Self-hate
Self-condemnation
Self-mutilation
Feeling Undeserving
Feeling of Unworthy
Feeling Second Rate

VIOLENCE

Feuding
Arguments
Physical Harm
Murder
Retaliation
Torture

WITCHCRAFT

Astrology
Black Magic
Mind-Reading
Palm-Reading
Talking to the Dead
Crystal Ball
Divination
ESP
Calling or Dispatching Demons
Fortune Telling
Tarot Cards
Horoscopes
Teleportation
Pendulum
Psychic Healing
Past Life Readings
Necromancy
Ouija Board
Levitation
Hypnosis
Read Occult and/or Witchcraft Books
Attended a Seance'
Sorcery
Voodoo

Other Books by Mary Hale:

The Formation of My Walls
The Walls of My Heart
The Castle of My Heart

Interested in having your
book published?
Contact APS Publishing

APS Books & More
2653 S. Lawndale
Chicago, IL 60623
847-942-6135
www.WeAreAPS.com

www.ingramcontent.com/pod-product-compliance
Lightning Source LLC
LaVergne TN
LVHW041347080426
835512LV00006B/651